SQL
PLSQL
ORACLE

SQL PLSQL ORACLE

ANDREW IGLA

Rev. date: 05/12/2016

To order additional copies of this book, contact:
Xlibris
1-800-455-039
www.Xlibris.com.au
Orders@Xlibris.com.au
740893

CONTENTS

Chapter 1: SQL 1

Chapter 2: PLSQL 25

Chapter 3: Oracle 53

This is a book about sql, plsql and Oracle. The first chapter is about SQL. The second chapter is about PLSQL and the third chapter is about Oracle.

Chapter 1

SQL

Let us say there is a table worker. To allow select, insert, update on table worker for user Andrew note the following.

SQL command.

Grant select, update, insert on worker to Andrew;

Let us say we wish to create a role in oracle. Note the following.

SQL command.

Create role Andrew_role;

Let us say we wish Andrew_role to select, update, insert to table worker. Note the following.

SQL command.

Grant select, update, insert on worker to Andrew_role;

Let us say we wish user Michael and Andrew to have the same privileges as Andrew_role on table worker. Note the following.

SQL command.

Grant Andrew_role to Andrew;
Grant Andrew_role to Michael;

Let us say we wish user Andrew to be connected to the database. Note the following.

SQL command.
Connect Andrew/newpassword;

Let us say we wish to create a sequence being a number getting bigger by one. Note the following.

SQL command.

Create sequence worker_ID
start with 100
increment by 1;

Let us say we wish to find the current value of the sequence worker_ID. Note the following.

SQL command.

Select worker_ID.currval
from dual;

Let us say we wish to find next value of sequence worker_ID. Note the following.

SQL command.

Select worker_ID.nextval
from dual;

Let us say we wish to create a table school. Note the following.

SQL command.

Create table school (
                        schoolname   varchar2(25),
                        teachername varchar2(25),
                        yearnumber   number,
                        hiredate   date);

Let us say we wish to create table address. Note the following.

SQL command.

Create table address(
                        sirname varchar2(25),
                        firstname varchar2(25),
                        address   varchar2(25));

Let us say we wish to create table worker with column links known as foreign keys to tables address and school. Note the following.

SQL command.

Create table worker(

```
worker_ID       number primary key,
last_name       varchar2(25) not null,
first_name      varchar2(25),
year_number     number,
teacher_name    varchar2(25) not null,
worktype        number(10, 2) default 10,
hire_date       date,
constraint a1
foreign key (teacher_name)
references school (teachername),
constraint a2
foreign key (last_name)
references address (sirname),
tablespace tables);
```

Let us say we wish to insert data into table worker. Note the following.

SQL command.

```
Insert into worker (worker_id, last_name,
first_name, teacher_name, worktype, hire_date)
values (worker_id.nextval, 'igla', 'andrew', 'mathsteacher', 20,
sysdate);
```

Let us say we wish to insert data in table address. Note the following.

SQL command.

Insert into address (sirname, firstname, address)
values ('igla', 'andrew', '76 orrong road');

Let us say we wish to insert into table school data. Note the following.

SQL command.

Insert into school(schoolname, teachername, yearnumber, hiredate)
values ('smithers college', 'mathsteacher', 7, sysdate-365);

Let us say we wish to select from table worker where hire date was more than thirty days ago.

SQL command.

Select first_name, last_name, teacher_name, year_number, hire_date
from worker
where hire_date < sysdate -30;

Let us say we wish to select data from table worker in a group by and order by manner. Note the following.

SQL command.

Select first_name, last_name, teacher_name, year_number,
tochar(hire_date,'yy-mm')
from worker
group by teacher_name,
order by year_number;

SQL output on computer screen.

	First name	Last name	teacher name	year number	date
row1	andrew	igla	maths teacher 6		'14-4'
row2	stewart	granger	maths teacher 7		'14-5'
row3	paul	newman	science teacher 3		'15-1'
row4	andrew	igla	science teacher 4		'15-6'

END SQL output.

Let us say we wish to select all columns from table worker all rows not with teacher_name equal to maths teacher. Note the following.

SQL command.

```
Select          *
from worker
where substr(teacher_name(1, 5)) <> 'maths';
```

The substr function selects the maths from maths teacher in the teacher_name column. The * character in the above sql statement selects all columns.

Let us say we wish to select all characters preceding English in column teacher_name in table school. Note the following.

SQL command.

```
Select teachername, yearnumber, hiredate
from school
where teachername like '%english teacher';
```

Even if indexes exist for table school no indexes can be used here.

Let us say we wish to select all characters after English in column teachername from table school. Note the following.

SQL command.

Select teachername, yearnumber, hiredate
from school
where teachername like 'english%';

An index is used for the above sql statement.

Let us say year number not equal to nine in column yearnumber in table school are selected. Note the following.

SQL command.

Select teachername, yearnumber
from school
where yearnumber <> 9;

Let us say column work type in table worker is added up for every teacher name type and displayed in numerical growing order of summation of work type. Note the following.

SQL command.

Select sum(work_type), teacher_name
from worker
group by teacher_name
order by sum(work_type);

SQL output from previous sql statement.

Sum(work_type)	teacher_name
20	english teacher
50	science teacher
100	maths teacher

SQL output finished.

Let from table worker the minimum of work type for each teacher name value ordered by growing numerical value of minimum work type values. Note the following.

Select min(work_type), teacher_name
from worker
group by teacher_name
order by min(work_type);

SQL output from previous sql statement

Min(work_type)	teacher_name
05	english teacher
07	science teacher
16	maths teacher

SQL output finished.

Select max(work_type), teacher_name
from worker
group by teacher_name
order by max(work_type);

SQL output from previous sql statement.

Max(work_type)	teacher_name
07	english teacher
08	science teacher
20	maths teacher

SQL output finished.

Select maximum work type from table worker for each teachername from table worker and order output display by maximum work type number in growing numerical value with column header of maximum for maximum work type number. Note the following.

Select max(work_type) maximum, teacher_name
from worker
group by teacher_name
order by max(work_type);

SQL output from previous sql statement.

maximum	teacher_name
07	english teacher
08	science teacher
20	maths teacher

SQL output finished.

Let the total columns of worker be listed when column teacher_name entries of table worker are in table school. The sub query of school table influence the main query of worker. Note the following.

Select *
from worker

Where teacher_name = (select teachername
                      From school);

Let last name, first name columns of table worker be selected when hire date was over thirty days ago and table address has the same value in the sir name column. Note the following.

SQL command.

        Select first_name, last_name
        from worker
        where last_name = (select sirname
                            from address
)
        and hire_date < sysdate-30;

The above sql statement uses a sub querry.

Let the columns of table worker be selected when column first name of table worker is null in value and teacher name column in table worker is in table school. Note the following.

SQL command.

Select first_name, last_name, teacher_name, yearnumber, worktype, hire_date
from worker
where first_name is null
and teacher_name = (select teachername
                        from school);

The above is a sub query statement in SQL.

Let the columns of table address be selected where exists worktype not equals twenty in table worker. Note the following.

SQL command.

Select sirname, firstname, address
from table address
where exists (select worktype
                from worker
                where worktype != 20);

Let the columns of table address be shown when last name sometimes is equal to Igla in table worker. Note the following.

SQL command.

Select sirname, firstname, address
from address
where exists (select last_name
                    from worker
                    last_name = 'IGLA');

Here in the above last name igla may not be in table address or it may be in table address but igla is definitely in table worker.

Let the columns of table address be shown when sirname not ever equal to IGLA. Note the following.

SQL command.

Select sirname, firstname, address
from address
where sirname not 'igla';

Let the columns of worker be selected where first name column is a null value. Note the following.

Select * from worker where first_name is null;

Let the columns of worker be selected where work type column equal to ten or twenty or thirty. Note the following.

SQL command.

```
select worker_id, last_name, first_name, teacher_name,
worktype, hire_date
from worker
where worktype in (10, 20, 30);
```

Let the columns of worker and school be displayed where column teacher_name of table worker and column teachername of table school are the same. Note the following

SQL command.

```
Select worker_id, last_name, first_name, teacher_name, worktype,
hire_date, schoolname, teachername, yearnumber, hiredate
from worker a, school b
where a.teacher_name = b.teachername;
```

The above SQL is a join sql statement.

Repeat the above with school name equal to smithers college.

SQL command.

```
Select worker_id, last_name, first_name, teacher_name, worktype,
hire_date, schoolname, teachername, yearnumber, hiredate
from worker a, school b
where a.teacher_name = b.teachername
and schoolname = 'smithers college';
```

The above SQL is a join sql statement.

In a sub querry sql statement where there are no indexes created two full table scans occur. Let us create two indexes. Note the following.

SQL command.

Create unique index teachername_worker on worker (teacher_name);

Create unique index teachername_school on school(teachername);

Let us again use a subquerry. Note the following.

SQL command.

Select first_name, last_name, teacher_name, yearnumber, worktype, hire_date
from worker
where first_name is null
and teacher_name = (select teachername
                    from school);

The above is a sub query statement in SQL.

Now with the two indexes a full table scan of table school happens and index teachername_worker is used for the above SQL statement.

Let the columns of worker and school be displayed where column teacher_name of table worker and column teachername of table school are the same. Note the following

SQL command.

Select worker_id, last_name, first_name, teacher_name, worktype, hire_date, schoolname, teachername, yearnumber, hiredate
from worker a, school b
where a.teacher_name = b.teachername;

This above sql statement is a join and with two indexes created on the previous page there is a full table scan for the second table mentioned in the join, table school, an index used for the first table of the join, table worker.

Repeating the above querry with a sql hint first rows note the following.

SQL command.

Select /* first_rows */

worker_id, last_name, first_name, teacher_name, worktype, hire_date, schoolname, teachername, yearnumber, hiredate
from worker a, school b
where a.teacher_name = b.teachername;

The above sql statement with first rows hint uses two indexes teachername_worker and teachername_school. If the two indexes were not here index row_id would be used for the join querry. In the above case no full table scans were used.

Let the above join sql statement be used where no data retrieved repeats itself. Note the following.

SQL command.

Select distinct
worker_id, last_name, first_name, teacher_name, worktype, hire_date, schoolname, teachername, yearnumber, hiredate
from worker a, school b
where a.teacher_name = b.teachername;

Let all rows of table worker and table school be displayed where teacher name entries are existing in both tables and where teacher name does not exist in both tables. Note the following.

SQL command.

Select worker_id, last_name, first_name, teacher_name, worktype, hire_date, schoolname, teachername, yearnumber, hiredate
from worker a, school b
where a.teacher_name = b.teachername (+);

The (+) symbol denotes the above outer join as this sql join is called.

Suppose we wish to create a table called temp1 with the previous sql statements data. Note the following.

SQL command.

Drop table temp1;

Create table temp1 as
Select worker_id, last_name, first_name, teacher_name, worktype, hire_date, schoolname, teachername, yearnumber, hiredate
from worker a, school b
where a.teacher_name = b.teachername (+);

Repeating the above querry with a sql hint rule note the following.

SQL command.

Select /* + rule */
worker_id, last_name, first_name, teacher_name, worktype,
hire_date, schoolname, teachername, yearnumber, hiredate
from worker a, school b
where a.teacher_name = b.teachername;

Indexes for both tables worker and school are used.

Let the previous join be used in the following way. Note the following.

SQL command.

Select worker_id, last_name, first_name, teacher_name, worktype,
hire_date, schoolname, teachername, yearnumber, hiredate
from worker a, school b
where a.teacher_name(+) = b.teachername;

Does a full table scan not using any indexes.

Let the previous join be used in the following way. Note the following.

SQL command.

Select worker_id, last_name, first_name, teacher_name, worktype, hire_date, schoolname, teachername, yearnumber, hiredate
from worker a, school b
where a.teacher_name = b.teachername;

Does a full table scan of the second table mentioned school and uses a index for worker even if a index was not created by the user. This would be the rowed index of table worker, row_id, when user not created index for table worker. The above sql statement is a normal join.

Note the following sub querry.

Select worker_id, last_name, first_name, teacher_name, worktype, hire_date, schoolname, teachername, yearnumber, hiredate
from worker a, school b
where exists (select /* +index(1a) */
             worker_Id
             from worker 1a, school 1b
                 where 1a.teacher_name<> 1b.teachername)
and a.teacher_name = b.teachername;

Table a above and table b not using indexes. Table 1a above using index rowID in the sub querry. Teacher names not the same for two tables, worker and school in this query.

Let us create bit map indexes. Note the following.

Create bitmap index worker_last_name_bit
on worker(last_name);

Create bitmap index work_type_bit
on worker(work_type);

Let us use these bit map indexes. Note the following.

SQL command.

Select /* index combine worker,
worker_last_name_bit, work_type_bit) */
Last_name, work_type
from worker
where work_type < 30
and last_name ='IGLA';

Bit map index conversion to row_id happens with the above SQL statement.

Let us create index for column work type in table worker. Note the following.

SQL command.

Create index worktype_idx   on worker(worktype);

Let us use the above index on a column worktype of table worker. Note the following.

SQL command.

Select /*+ index(worker, worktype_idx) */   * from worker;

Oracle parallel querry allows you to set the degree of parallelism to the number of cpu's on your server minus one. Let us do a join parallel querry. Note the following.

Select /* + use merge(a, b)   parallel (a, 4) parallel (b, 4) */
Last_name, schoolname
from worker a, school b
where a.teacher_name = b.teacher_name;

Let the columns last name, first name, address of table address be displayed where address not 76 orrong road and last name not igla and the condition exists where first name not Andrew and work type not equal to ten where last name same in both tables address and worker. Note the following.

SQL command.

Select b1.lastname, b1.firstname, b1.address
from worker a1, address b1
where exists (select a2.lastname
                from address a2, worker b2
                where a2.lastname = b2.last_name
                and a2.firstname not in 'Andrew'
                and worktype != 10)
and b1.address != '76 orrong road'
and b1.lastname <> 'Igla';

This is a join sql statement with a where exists sub query containing a join.

Chapter 2

PLSQL

Let the following be a PLSQL statement block. Note the following.

```
Declare
/* declare local variables */
nworktype     number(10) := 30;
nfirstname    varchar2(10) := 'andrew';
nlastname     varchar2(10) := 'Igla';
ntimedate     date;
Begin
/* update the worker table */
update worker
set worktype = nworktype
where first_name = nfirstname
and last_name = nlastname;
/* check to see if the record was found for the previous update
where and and clause. */
if SQL%NOTFOUND then
insert into worker (id, first_name, last_name, worktype,
teacher_name, year_number, hire_date)
(worker_sequence.NEXTVAL, nfirstname, nlastname, nworktype,
'maths teacher', 11, sysdate -60);
end if;
end;
```

The above is an example of PLSQL code.

Let us enter in table counter fifty rows of sequential numbers. Note the following PLSQL code block.

```
Declare
nloopcounter  BINARY_INTEGGER := 1;
Begin
loop
insert into counter (count)
/* counter is a table with one column count */
values (nloopcounter);
nloopcounter := nloopcounter+1;
exit when nloopcounter > 50;
end loop;
End;
```

New PLSQL code block.

```
Declare
nloopcounter BINARY_INTEGER := 0;
nworktype        number(10);
nfirstname       varchar2(10);
nlastname        varchar2(10);
nteachername   varchar2(10);
cursor cworker is
select first_name, last_name, worktype, teacher_name
from worker
where hire_date > sysdate -365;
begin
open cworker;
```

```
loop
fetch cworker into nfirstname, nlastname, nworktype,
nteachername;
exit when cworker%NOTFOUND;
insert into temp2 (first_name, last_name, worktype, teacher_
name) values (nfirstname, nlastname, nworktype, nteachername);
nloopcounter := nloopcounter+1;
end loop;
close cworker;
end;
```

The sql fetch went into temp2 table until no more data from table worker for the period of the last year.

Let us create temporary table addresstemp3. Note the following.

SQL command.

```
Create addresstemp3 (lastname  varchar2(25),
                firstname  varchar2(25),
                address  varchar2(25),
                task  varchar2(25),
                counter    number)
                tablespace tables;
```

Let us create temporary table schooltemp4. Note the following.

SQL command.

Create schooltemp4 (schoolname varchar2(25),
                    teachername varchar2(25),
                    lastname varchar2(25),
                    firstname varchar2(25),
                    task   varchar2(25),
                    counter   number)
                    tablespace tables;

Let us create a non unique index on lastname for table schooltemp4. Note the following.

SQL command.

Create index school_lastname_idx on table schooltemp4(lastname)
          tablespace indexes;

All tables are created in table space tables. All indexes are created in a separate table space from where tables are. This would be table space indexes.

Create table school (
                    schoolname   varchar2(25),
                    teachername varchar2(25),
                    firstname   varchar(25),
                    lastname   varchar(25),
          hiredate   date);

Let us note that in table address the same last name and first name can have more than one address. Let us note that in table school the same last name and first name can have more than one school. We wish to enter in column task, of table addresstemp3, if in table address first name and last name is already there in table address the characters 'no insert required table address'. We wish to enter in column task the characters 'future insert in column address required' if no match exists in table address with column. lastname and first name. Let us create the following PLSQL trigger. Note the following PLSQL block.

```
Create or replace trigger boundaryaddress
before insert or update on worker
for each row
declare
n_lastname    varchar2(25);
n_firstname   varchar2(25);
n_address     varchar2(25);
n_temptask    varchar(100);
n_counter     number := 0;
cursor caddress is
select firstname, sirname, address
from address
where lastname = :new.last_name
and firstname = :new.first_name;
begin
open caddress;
loop
fetch caddress into n_firstname, n_lastname, n_address;
```

If caddress%NOTFOUND   then

if n_counter = 0   then

insert into addresstemp3 (firstname, lastname, address, task, counter)

values (:new.first_name, :new.last_name, null, 'future insert table address required', n_counter);

/* address column of table addresstemp3 a null character :new.address does not exist mistake fixed bug fixed, :new.firstname does not exist but :new.first_name exits, bug fixed. Pointing out traps for programmers here, correct column names table worker. */

end if;

exit;

else

n_counter := n_counter+1;

insert into addresstemp3(firstname, lastname, address, task, counter)

values (n_lastname, n_firstname, n_address, 'No insert into table address reqired of :new.last_name etc as already same data in table address.', n_counter);

end if;

end loop;

end boundaryaddress;

The above PLSQL trigger refers to ':new.firstname : new.lastname'. This refers to the new column entries in table worker noted at the begining of the trigger by 'before insert or update of worker'.

Let us note that in table school the same last name and first name can have more than one school. We wish to enter in column task, in table schooltemp4, if in table school first name and last name is already there the characters 'no insert required table school first name and last name already in table school'. We wish to enter in column task the characters 'future insert in table school required if no match exists in table school with column lastname and first name'. Let us create the following PLSQL trigger. Note the following PLSQL block.

```
Create or replace trigger boundaryschool
before insert or update of worker
for each row
declare
n_schoolname   varchar2(25);
n_teachername  varchar2(25);
n_lastname     varchar2(25);
n_firstname    varchar2(25);
n_counter      number;
cursor cschool is
select schoolname, teachername, lastname, firstname
from school
where lastname = :new.last_name
and firstname = :new.first_name;
```

```
begin
open cschool;
loop
fetch cschool into n_schoolname, n_teachername, n_lastname,
n_firstname;
if cschool%NOTFOUND    then
if n_counter = 0  then
insert into schooltemp4 (schoolname, teachername, firstname,
lastname, task, counter)
values (null, :new.teacher_name, :new.first_name,
:new.last_name, 'future insert into table school with :new values
from insert or update of table worker', n_counter); end if;
exit;
else
n_counter := n_counter +1;
insert into schooltemp4(schoolname, teachername, firstname,
lastname, task, counter)
values (n_schoolname, n_teachername, n_firstname, n_lastname,
'no insert table school required', n_counter);
end if;
end loop;
end boundaryschool;
```

```
Create or replace trigger boundaryworker1
before insert or update of school
for each row
declare
n_first_name    varchar2(25);
n_last_name     varchar2(25);
n_teacher_name  varchar2(25);
n_year_number   number;
n_hire_date     date;
n_counter       number := 0;
cursor cworker is
select first_name, last_name, teacher_name, hire_date
from worker
where last_name = :new.lastname
and first_name = :new.firstname;
begin
open cworker;
loop
fetch cworker into n_first_name, n_last_name, n_teacher_name,
n_hire_date;
/* fetching row in table worker where last name and first name
same as table school, prior to insert or update of table school.*/
if cworker%NOTFOUND  then
if n_counter = 0 then /*first time data notfound table worker tofix*/
insert into workertemp5(first_name, last_name, teacher_name,
hire_date, task, counter)
values (:new.first_name, :new.last_name, null, null, 'future insert
into table worker needed of table school name entry', n_counter);
```

```
end if;
exit;
else
n_counter := n_counter+1;
insert into workertemp5 (first_name, last_name, teacher_name,
hire_date, task, counter)
values (n_first_name, n_last_name, n_teacher_name, n_hire_
date, 'no update or insert of table worker required, table worker
has data from table school new insert or update', n_counter);
end if;
end loop;
end boundaryworker1;
```

End trigger, insert or update of table school next.

```
Create or replace trigger boundaryworker2
before insert or update of address
for each row
declare
n_first_name    varchar2(25);
n_last_name    varchar2(25);
n_teacher_name  varchar2(25);
n_year_number   number;
n_hire_date       date;
n_counter          number := 0;
cursor cworker is
select first_name, last_name, teacher_name, hire_date
from worker
where last_name = :new.sirname
and first_name = :new.firstname;
/* :new.sirname :new.firstname comes from data of insert or
update to table address */
begin
open cworker;
loop
fetch cworker into n_first_name, n_last_name, n_teacher_name,
n_hire_date;
/* fetching row in table worker where last name and first name
same as intending insert to table address, column sirname and
firstname,.*/
```

```
if cworker%NOTFOUND  then
if n_counter = 0 then /* data not ever found in table worker */
insert into workertemp5(first_name, last_name, teacher_name,
hire_date, task, counter)
values (  :new.first_name, :new.last_name, null, null, 'new
columns of firstname and sirname from intending insert into table
address too need to be inserted in table worker', n_counter);
end if;
exit;
else
n_counter := n_counter+1;
insert into workertemp5 (first_name, last_name, teacher_name,
hire_date, task, counter)
values (n_first_name, n_last_name, n_teacher_name, n_hire_date,
'no update or insert of table worker required, data from new insert
or update to table address already in table worker', n_counter);
end if;
end loop;
end boundaryworker2;
```

So PLSQL triggers have been covered. Let us examine PLSQL procedures. Note the following.

Create table task (username   varchar2(25),
                   password   varchar2(25),
                   task   varchar2(25),
                   counter   number)
                   tablespace tables;

Create or replace procedure test1
                   (**n_user   IN varchar2(25),**
                        n_password   IN varchar2(25),
                        n_counter   OUT number
)
                   IS
             n_localtask   varchar2(100);
begin
        n_counter := 0; /* n_counter assigned value here first time in procedure test1 */
if n_user = 'andrew'   then
             if n_password = 'igla' then
             connect Andrew/igla;
             grant select, insert, update on worker to andrew;
             n_counter := n_counter +1; /*returning non zero value*/
n_localtask := 'granted select update insert user to table worker';
insert into task (username, password, task, counter)
        values (n_user, n_password, n_localtask, n_counter);
        end if;
end if;
end test1;   /* end of procedure test1 */

Create table temp2 (task varchar2(100), counter number);

The following is the PLSQL block that calls up procedure test1.

```
Declare
n_user  varchar2(25);
n_password  varchar2(25);
n_counter     number;     /* n_counter not assigned in value */
        /* n_counter OUT parameter in procedure test1 */
begin
n_user := 'Andrew';
n_password := 'igla';
test1(n_user, n_password, n_counter);
/* calling of procedure test1, n_counter not assigned value in
entry to test1 procedure. */
if n_counter > 0 then
insert into temp2 (task, counter)
values ('procedure test1 worked', n_counter);
/* n_counter assigned in value in test1 procedure, used to
enter columns in table task in procedure test1 and table temp2
in current PLSQL block, has the same numeric value for both
tables. */
end if;
end;
```

```
Create or replace procedure test2
                (       n_user          IN varchar2(25),
                        n_password  IN varchar2(25),
                        n_counter      IN OUT number
                )
        IS
                n_localtask    varchar2(100);
/* no need to assign value here to n_counter as INOUT defined. */
begin
if n_user = 'michael'    then
        if n_password = 'igla' then
        connect michael/igla;
        grant select, insert, update on worker to michael;
        n_counter := n_counter +1;

else    /* inner if statement linked here, igla not n_password. */
else    /* n_user not michael */
n_localtask := 'grant select update insert user to table worker';
        insert into task (username, password, task, counter)
        values (n_user, n_password, n_localtask, n_counter);
end if;
end if;
        end test2;                    /* end of procedure test2 */
/*Try the same routine above with PLSQL statement 'if x and y
then', */
```

The following is the PLSQL block that calls up procedure test2.

```
Declare
n_user  varchar2(25);
n_password  varchar2(25);
n_counter     number;
begin
n_counter := 0;    /* n_counter assigned value here and is this
value entering test2 procedure */
n_user := 'michael';
n_password := 'igla';
test2(n_user, n_password, n_counter);
/* calling of procedure test2. */
if n_counter  > 0  then
insert into temp2 (task, counter)
values ('procedure test2 worked', n_counter);
/* n_counter assigned in value in test2 procedure, used to
enter columns in table task in procedure test2 or table temp2
in current PLSQL block and has the same numeric value for
both tables. */
end if;
end;
```

```
Create or replace procedure test3
is
    n_firstname      varchar2(25);
    n_lastname       varchar2(25);
cursor ctest3  is
select lastname, firstname
from worker
where teachername = 'mathsteacher'; begin
open ctest3;
loop
fetch into n_lastname, n_firstname;
if  ctest3%NOTFOUND    then
exit;      /* no more records for maths teacher being column
teachername */
else
select firstname, lastname, teachername /* link to label q */
from school
where teachername = 'mathsteacher'
and firstname = n_firstname
and lastname = n_lastname;
if SQL%NOTFOUND then          /* label q, no cursor sql here */
insert into school (firstname, lastname, teachername)
values (n_firstname, n_lastname, 'mathsteacher');
end if;
end if;
end loop;
end test3;
```

All records with teacher name equal to maths teacher are retrieved from table worker and table school is checked as having these records and if not these records are inserted in table school.

The following is a PLSQL block that calls procedure test3 a self contained procedure not requiring parameters.

Declare
begin
test3;
end;

Consider a new test3 procedure called test4. Note the following.

```
Create or replace procedure test4
(
    n_firstname   IN   varchar2(25),
    n_lastname    IN   varchar2(25)
)
IS
begin
Select firstname, lastname
from school
where firstname = n_firstname
and lastname = n_lastname
and teachername = 'mathsteacher';
if sql%NOTFOUND then
insert into school (firstname, lastname, teachername)
values (n_firstname, n_lastname, 'mathsteacher');
end if;
end test4;  /* end of test4 procedure */
```

This is the PLSQL block that calls procedure test4. Note the following.

Below is a PLSQL block calling procedures test4 and test5. Note the following.

```
Declare
n_lastname  varchar2(25);
n_firstname  varchar2(25);
begin
cworker is
select lastname, firstname       /* procedure entry info done here. */
from worker
where teachername = 'mathsteacher';
open cworker;
loop
fetch cworker into n_lastname, n_firstname;
if  cworker%NOTFOUND    then
exit;
end if;
test4(n_firstname, n_lastname);

test5(n_firstname, n_lastname);

/* main PLSQL block calling procedures test4 and test5. */
end loop;
end; /* end PLSQL block calling test4 and test5 */
```

Procedure test5 called to insert last name and first name into table address, if not already in table address, when last name and first name in table worker originally.

```
Create or replace procedure test5
(
    n_firstname   IN   varchar2(25),
    n_lastname    IN   varchar2(25)
)
IS
begin
Select firstname, lastname
from address
where firstname = n_firstname
and lastname = n_lastname;
if sql%NOTFOUND then
insert into address (firstname, lastname, address)
values (n_firstname, n_lastname, '76 orrong road');
end if;
end test5;  /* end of test5 procedure */
```

On the previous pages a PLSQL block calls procedures test4 and test5 together in a PLSQL block. Oracle provides a package set up in PLSQL to do this. Consider a PLSQL package and a PLSQL block calling the PLSQL package. Note the following.

In a PLSQL package there is a header package and body of the package holding related procedures to be executed together in a PLSQL block. Here is the PLSQL header package not body of the package.

Create or replace   Package test
as
procedure test4(firstname varchar2(25), lastname varchar2(25));
procedure test5(firstname varchar2(25), lastname varchar2(25));
end test;

The above is known as the package header. Usually procedures are called together or are related in a package.

Here is the PLSQL package body code. Note the following.

```
Create or replace package body test
AS
procedure test4
(
      n_firstname   IN   varchar2(25),
      n_lastname    IN   varchar2(25)
)
IS
begin
Select firstname, lastname
from school
where firstname = n_firstname
and lastname = n_lastname
and teachername = 'mathsteacher';
if sql%NOTFOUND then
insert into school (firstname, lastname, teachername)
values (n_firstname, n_lastname, 'mathsteacher');
end if;
end test4;  /* end of test4 procedure in package test. */
```

/*PLSQL package BODY test code continued here */

```
procedure test5
(
     n_firstname   IN   varchar2(25),
     n_lastname    IN   varchar2(25)
)
IS
begin
Select firstname, lastname
from address
where firstname = n_firstname
and lastname = n_lastname;
if sql%NOTFOUND then
insert into address (firstname, lastname, address)
values (n_firstname, n_lastname, '76 orrong road');
end if;
end test5;  /* end of PLSQL test5 procedure package body code */

end test;   /* end PLSQL package body code */
```

/* The above is the package body containing two procedures test4 and test5. */

The following is a PLSQL block calling procedures in package test. Note the following.

```
Declare
firstname   varchar2(25);
lastname    varchar2(25);
begin
call test.test4('Andrew', 'igla');

/* Package test, internal package procedure test4 called */

Call  test.test5('andrew', 'igla');

/* package test, internal package procedure test5 called */

End;
```

PLSQL supports PLSQL functions. Note the following.


```
Create or replace function workerA
(worktype          number,
lastname           varchar2(25))
return             varchar2(25);
begin
if           worktype = 30 then
return                'Igla'; /* returning varchar2(25) */
else
      return 'not igla';
end     workerA;
```

Chapter 3

Oracle

Let us look at Oracle issues now.

Data types.

Char up to 2,000 bytes fixed length character field.

VARCHAR2 variable length character field up t0 4,000 characters in length.

Date 7 byte field stores dates dd-mon-yy.

Number variable length number column assigned number.

Long 2 times gigabytes in length.

Creation of table worker, note the following.

```
Create table worker(
worker_ID       number primary key,
last_name       varchar2(25)    not null,
first_name      varchar2(25),
year_number     number,
teacher_name    varchar2(25) not null,
worktype        number(10, 2) default 10,
hire_date       date,
constraint a1
foreign key (teacher_name)
references school (teachername),
constraint a2
foreign key  (last_name)
references address (sirname),
tablespace tables);
```

Let us create a non unique index on column teachername of table worker in table space indexes.

SQL command.

Create nonunique index teachername_worker on worker (teachername) tablespaces indexes;

Let us create a view based on table worker. Views contain no data and can not have an index attached to it. When a null is detected in column worktype in table worker a zero is inserted in the view. This last sentence is to explain the NVL function in the SQL statement. Note the following.

SQL command.

Create view worker_view (firstname, sirname, Id, worktype)
as
select first_name, last_name, worker_id, NVL(worktype, 0)
from worker;

To drop the view worker_view note the following.

SQL command.

Drop view worker_view;

Let us drop column date from table worker. Note the following.

SQL command.

alter table worker drop column date;

Let a column called date be marked as not used. The column will be dropped later. Note the following.

SQL command.

Alter table worker set unused column date;

Let us drop unused columns in table worker. Note the following.

SQL command.

Alter table worker drop unused columns;

Let us create a database. Note the following.

SQL command.

Create database LINK.databasename
connect to system identified by manager using databasename;

Let us create an oracle object. Note the following.

SQL command.

Create or replace type worker_eg
as   object   (firstname   varchar2(25),
                             lastname   varchar2(25),
                             teachername varchar2(25),
                             worktype   number);

Let us create a view. Note the following.

SQL command.

Create view workerview of worker
as
select firstname, lastname, teachername, worktype
from worker;

The SQL command rollback allows users to take the database to a version of the last commit SQL command given. A table space can have many rollback segments. Note the following.

SQL command.

Rollback;

Let us create a rollback segment segment_worker. Note the following.

SQL command.

Create rollback segment segment_ worker;

Oracle has a system rollback segement in the system table space. Oracle has a second rollback segment in the system table space. Oracle has a RBS table space for many production data base rollback segments. Oracle has many rollback segments in the RBS table space. Note the following.

SQL command.

Create rollback segment production1 tablespace RBS;

Let us drop a roll back segment. Note the following.

SQL command.

Drop rollback segment production1;

Let us activate a roll back segment or enable the roll back segment. Note the following.

SQL command.

Alter rollback segment production1 online;

Let us disable a roll back segment. Note the following.

SQL command.

Alter rollback segment production1 offline;

Use the set transaction command to specify which rollback segment is used till the next SQL commit statement storing the sql statements before the commit statement in the roll back segment. Note the following.

SQL command.

Set transaction use rollback segment productionA;
insert into temp
select * from worker;

Commit;

Let us create a practical rollback segment. Note the following.

SQL command.

Create rollback segment productionA tablespace RBS storage (optimal 2250k);

Let us create table worker1. Note the following.

SQL command.

```
Create table worker1(
worker_ID      number primary key,
last_name      varchar2(25)   not null,
first_name     varchar2(25),
year_number    number,
teacher_name   varchar2(25),
worktype       number(10, 2),
hire_date      date,
constraint a1
foreign key (worktype)
references temp4 (worktype),
tablespace tables);
```

Oracle has partitions to distribute the I/O load for large tables. Partitioning uses the foreign key of the table being partitioned. Range partitioning is about ranges of the foreign key column of the table being partitioned, in this case column worktype.

Let us create a table with range partitioning called worker1. Note the following.

SQL command.

Create table worker1(

worker_ID   number primary key,

last_name   varchar2(25)   not null,

first_name   varchar2(25),

year_number   number,

teacher_name varchar2(25),

worktype   number(10, 2),

hire_date   date,

constraint a1

foreign key (worktype)

references temp4 (worktype))

partition by range (worktype)

(partition partA values less than (30)

tablespace partA_TS

partition partB values less than (MAXVALUE)

tablespace partB_TS);

Let us query directly from a partitioned table of the above. Note the following.

SQL command.

Select * from worker1 partition (partB) where worktype between 10 and 50;

Let us create an index for a partitioned table worker1 Table worker1 has two partitions named partA and partB. The following key word local tells oracle to create a separate index for each of the two partitions. Note the following.

SQL command.

```
Create index worker1_worktype
on worker1(worktype)
local
(partition PartA     tablespace partA_ndx_TS,
partition PartB      tablespace partB_ndx_TS);
```

Let us create an index for the partitioned table worker1 not using key word local but key word global. A global index may contain values of column worktype from multiple partitions. The global clause in this create index command allows ranges of the worktype column different to their ranges in the create partition table command. Note the following.

SQL command.

```
Create index worker1_worktype on worker1(worktype)
global partition by range (worktype)
(partition partA values less than (100)
tablespace partA_ndx_TS,
partition partB values less than (MAXVALUE)
tablespace partB_ndx_TS);
```

The following is hash partitioning. Note the following.

SQL command.

```
Create table worker1(
worker_ID      number primary key,
last_name      varchar2(25)   not null,
first_name     varchar2(25),
year_number    number,
teacher_name   varchar2(25),
worktype       number(10, 2),
hire_date      date,
constraint a1
foreign key (worktype)
references temp4 (worktype))
partition by hash (worktype)
(partition partA
tablespace partA_TS
partition partB
tablespace partB_TS);
```

If no specific storage parameters are given in the create table, create index, create rollback segment command then the database will use the storage parameters of the create tablespace command given earlier. A number of extents make up a segment of memory. A segment of memory grows with more extents. An extent has blocks of memory.

The storage parameters specify the initial extent size, the next extent size and the pctincrease size. The initial extent size is the size of memory of the initial extent.   The next extent size is the second extent size of memory. Pctincrease is the dilation factor the next extent is multiplied to create the next extent size of memory. Each block of memory has unused memory by oracle and is based on PCTFREE magnification in the storage parameters of create table, create index, create rollback segment and create table space command.

A data base can have multiple users each user with a schema, collection of tables and indexes.

Let us examine the synonym command. Note the following.

SQL command.

Create public synonym worker for Andrew.worker;

The owner of the table worker is Andrew and the public can now refer to table Andrew.worker with worker. A synonym provides referals to tables, views, procedures, functions, packages and sequences.

Let us reclaim table worker memory space except the initial memory space in the storage parameters. Note the following.

SQL command.

Truncate table worker drop storage;

Let us create 100 megabytes of memory in table space Andrew_TS for user Andrew. Note the following.

SQL command.

Alter user Andrew
quota 100M on Andrew_TS;

Let us create a data file for table space worker_TS starting with a segment memory size of 10 megabytes increasing by 10 megabytes multiplied by a dilation 12 percent keeping 20 percent memory space in the memory segment free space and a file size of 500 megabytes of memory. Note the following.

SQL command.

Create tablespace worker_TS
datafile '/ tblworker07.dbf' size 500 m
default storage (initial 10M next 10m pctincrease 12 pctfree 20);

Let us delete all records of table worker without reclaiming memory space that worker table occupies as free space. Note the following.

SQL command.

Truncate table worker reuse storage;

Let us delete all records of table worker in partition part_worker reclaiming memory space of the part_worker partition as a free memory space. Note the following.

SQL   command.

Alter table worker truncate partition part_worker drop storage;

Let us delete all records from table worker in setting free memory used by table worker except the initial extent size of memory of the segment of memory of table worker. Note the following.

SQL command.

Truncate table worker drop storage;

Let us add a new data file to table space worker_TS with file storage parameters allowing expansion to 400 megabytes. Note the following.

SQL command.

Alter tablespace worker_TS
add datafile '/ db07.dbf' size 100M autoextend on maxsize 400m;

To reclaim the unusable space of an index larger memory space than storage parameter size here use the alter index rebuild command having an initial 10 megabytes increasing by 5Megabytes expanding by 10 percent keeping 10 percent free. Note the following.

SQL command.

Alter index worker_index rebuild
storage   (initial 10M
                    next 5M
                    pctincrease 10
                    pctfree 10)
tablespace indexes;

Let us extend a database data file to 200 megabytes of memory expanding to 400megabytes. Note the following.

SQL command.

alter database datafile '/db01.dbf' resize 200M
autoextend on   nextsize 20M maxsize 400M;

Let us alter table space andrew_TS as consisting of temporary segments. Note the following.

SQL command.

Alter tablespace Andrew_TS temporary;

Let us create table space andrew_TS consisting of temporary segments of memory. Note the following.

SQL command.

Create tablespace andrew_TS temporary;

Let us alter table space worker_TS as permament to store permament tables or indexes like table worker. Note the following.

SQL command.

Alter tablespace worker_TS permament;

Let us create tablespace worker_TS as a permament. Note the following.

SQL command.

Create tablespace Andrew_TS permament;

When a segment of memory is dropped its extents are free to combine to new memory. Oracle combines free extents in table space worker_TS. Note the following.

SQL command.

alter tablespace worker_TS coalesce;

Let us extend a data file by 20 mega bytes up to 200 mega bytes, via the alter database command. Note the following.

SQL command.

alter database datafile '/db01.dbf' resize 200M
autoextend on
nextsize   20M
maxsize   size 200M;

Let us grant to user Andrew select on all columns and update on columns id and last_name all on table worker. Note the following.

SQL command.

grant select, update (id, last_name) on worker to Andrew;

Let us grant select on all columns and update on columns teachername and yearnumber all on table school for user Andrew along with the ability to grant the same to other users. Note the following.

SQL command.
grant select, update (teachername, yearnumber) on school to andrew with grant option;

Let us revoke update on columns last_name and worker_id on table worker from user andrew. Note the following.

SQL command.

revoke update (last_name, worker_id) on worker from andrew;

Let us drop user andrew from the oracle database. Note the following.

SQL command.

drop user andrew cascade;

Let us create a table space Andrew_TS. Note the following.

SQL Command.

create tablespace Andrew_TS;

Let us revoke on table worker select privileges for user andrew. Note the following.

SQL command.

revoke select on worker from user andrew;

Let us change index indexA2 table space name to andrewindex _TS with an initial size of 20megabyte extent increasing with 10megabyte extent with no memory extent magnification. Note the following.

SQL command.

Alter index indexA2 rebuild tablespace andrewindex_TS storage (initial 20M next 10M pctincrease 0);

Let us grant select on all columns and update on column worker_id and last_name on table worker to all users in public. Note the following.

SQL command.

Grant select, update (worker_id, last_name) on worker to public;

Let us grant select and update on table worker to all users in public with same grant privileges to new users. Note the following.

SQL command.

grant select, update (worker_id, last_name) on worker to public with grant option;

Let us revoke delete privileges on table worker for user andrew. Note the following.

SQL command.

revoke delete on worker from andrew;

Let us revoke all data base object privileges from table worker for user andrew. Note the following.

SQL command.

revoke all on worker from andrew;

Let us create an oracle role with log in to data base or session creation. Note the following.

SQL command.

create role   a1;
grant create session to a1;

Let us create an Oracle role with select and insert privileges to table worker owned by user andrew. Note the following.

SQL command.

create role a2;
grant select, insert on andrew.worker to a2;

Let us grant Oracle role a1 to Oracle role a2. Note the following.

SQL command.

grant a1 to a2;

Let us grant Oracle role a2 to user Michael. Note the following.

SQL command.

Grant a2 to Michael;

Let us grant everything above to user leo with the ability to grant and revoke these same privileges to a final user destination. Note the following.

SQL command.

Grant a2 to leo with adminoption;

Let us create oracle role creator. Note the following.

SQL command.

Create role creator;

Let us grant create session and create user and alter user to role creator. Role creator can log in to database.

SQL command.

Grant create session, create user, alter user to creator;

Let us create a default role for user Andrew as connect. By default user Andrew can log in to data base. Note the following.

SQL command.

Alter user Andrew default role connect;

Let a user Andrew have all oracle roles except oracle role creator. Note the following.

SQL command.

alter user andrew default role all except creator;

Let us unlock account for user Andrew. Note the following.

SQL command.

Alter user Andrew account unlock;

Without allocating memory to a table space a user can not create a table or index. As already explained the alter user quota command must be given first.

Let us create a user not able to create tables or indexes because no memory space allocated to table space Andrew_TS. Note the following.

SQL command.

Create user Andrew identified by igla default tablespace Andrew_TS temporary tablespace temp;

Let us prescribe the maximum amount of login attempts as four. Note the following.

SQL command.

create profile andrew_profile limit FAILED_LOGINATTEMPTS 4;

Let us create user Andrew with password igla with the above profile andrew_profile. Also let user Andrew have create session privileges. Note the following.

SQL command.

Create user Andrew identified by igla profile andrew_profile; grant create session to andrew;

If there are four failed connects to the database oracle locks the account. Note the following.

1) Connect andrew/wrongpassword

2) connect andrew/wrongpassword

3) connect andrew/wrongpassword

4) connect andrew/wrongpassword

5) connect Andrew/rightpassword

System responds account is locked.

Let us unlock the account now. Note the following.

SQL command.

alter user andrew account unlock;

Let us grant SYSOPER or SYSDBA privileges to user Andrew for performing database administrator functions. Note the following.

SQL command.

Connect Andrew as sysdba;

Let us revoke oracle dba privileges from user andrew. Note the following.

SQL command.

revoke SYSDBA from andrew;

Let us expire user andrew's password. This is not a drop user name sql command. Note the following.

alter user andrew password expire;

When user Andrew attempts next to login. Note the following.

Connect Andrew/igla

Oracle responds with the following, response start.

account has expired.

Changing password for Andrew.

Old password: type in old password.

New password: type in new password.

Retype new password: type in new password.

Password changed.

Connected.

response above end.

Snapshots are created in the local database and pull data from the remote master database. The user creating the snapshot must have create snapshot privileges assigned to the same user. The snaps table space must be created already. *There are two kinds of snapshots simple returning a row of data from a remote table each time and complex snapshot returning a join or group by sql set of rows from a remote data base.*

The snapshot command contains a refresh complete clause indicating it should be completely be recreated each time the snapshot command is used.

To query a remote database as in a snapshot you must first create a remote database link. Let us create a database link to a remote database. Note the following.

SQL command.

create public database link andrew_link connect to Andrew identified by igla using 'IG';

The service name is IG.

Let us select from remote database table worker using the remote database link Andrew_link. This is not a snapshot here yet. Note the following.

SQL command.

Select * from worker@andrew_link;

A shared database link uses shared server connections to support the database link connections. Let us create a shared database link to the remote database for user andrew. Note the following.

SQL command.

Create public database link Andrew_link_shared connect to Andrew identified by Igla using 'IG';

Now that the remote database link is created first importantly we are ready to create a snapshot. Two remote database links Andrew_link or Andrew_link_shared can be used here. Note the following.

SQL command.

```
Create snapshot worker_count
        pctfree 5
        tablespace snap
        refresh complete
start with sysdate
next sysdate + 7
storage (initial 50k next 50k pctincrease 0)
as select worker_id, lastname, count(*)
from Andrew.worker@andrew_link
group by lastname;
```

Let us now drop the snapshot worker_count. Note the following.

SQL command.

Drop snapshot worker_count;

Table column constraints can not happen for a snapshot. You can change storage parameters of a snapshot. In the create snapshot command previously pctfree was equal to 5. Let us now set pctfree to 20. Note the following.

SQL command.

Alter snapshot worker_count pctfree 20;

A snapshot log is a table that maintains a record of modifications to the master table in a snapshot, for simple snapshots only. Let us create a snapshot log. Note the following.

SQL command.

Create snapshot log on worker
table space log_b
storage (initial 100k next 50k pctincrease 0)
pctfree 5 pctused 80;

Let us create a change in pctfree of snapshot log. Note the following.

SQL command.

Alter snapshot log worker pctfree 10;

Let us drop a snapshot log. Note the following.

SQL command.

Drop snapshot log on worker;

Dynamically alter the instance to use a different resource allocation plan via the set initial_consumer_group clause of the alter system command. Create a resource plan for your daytime users and another resource plan for batch users. The resource allocation plan for the instance will thus be altered without needing to shut down the instance and then restating the instance. Note the following.

SQL command.

alter system set initial_consumer_group = 'DAYTIME_USERS';
alter system set initial_consumer_group = 'BATCH_USERS';

A stored outline stores a set of hints for a querry. To start creating hints for all queries set the   CREATE_STORED _OUTLINES in the INIT.ORA file to true. All of the outlines will be stored in a default category or development category. Use the create outline command to create an outline for a query. Note the following.

SQL command.

Create outline worker_count for category development on select count(*) from worker where firstname = 'ANDREW';

Let us change the category of outline worker_count to default from development, such as a development data base not production database. Note the following.

SQL command.

alter outline worker_count change category to default;

Perform physical file backups of a database while the database is running if archivelog mode is used by the database. Oracle writes to the online redo log files, irrespectively of physical file back ups, overwriting them when the maximum number of redo log files are full. *The archivelog background process makes a copy of each redo log file before over writing it.*

Place data base in archivelog mode. Note the following.

Svrngr1
connect internal as sysdba
startup mount cc1;
alter database archivelog;
archivelog start;
alter database open;

Let us create two oracle views. Note the following.

SQL command.

create or replace worker_view as
select ID, lastname
from worker
where ID > 10
and   ID < 100;

create view workerb_view
as
select ID, worktype, lastname
from worker
group by work type;

Let us create a function in Oracle. Note the following.

SQL command.

```
Create or replace function
Insert_tempworker (p_ID IN worker.ID%TYPE)
return worker.ID%TYPE
AS
Begin
insert into temp (ID, sirname)
values (p_ID, 'IGLA');
return p_ID;
end insert_tempworker;
```

Let us create the PLSQL block to call function insert_tempworker listed before. Note the following.

SQL command.

```
Declare
1local_ID      number;
2local_ID      number;
begin
1local_id := 80;
call insert_tempworker(1local_ID) into :2local_ID;
end;
```

Let us create an oracle function. Note the following.

```
Create or replace function
f_lastname (v_ID IN worker.ID%TYPE)
return varchar2
as
v_result varchar2(50);
begin
select lastname
into v_result
from worker
where ID = v_ID;
return v_result;
end f_lastname;
```

Let us call the function called f_lastname from a PLSQL block. Note the following.

SQL command.

```
Declare
local_ID    worker.ID%TYPE;
v_resultend varchar2(50);
begin
local_ID := 30;
call f_lastname (Local_ID)
into :v_resultend;
end;
```

Let the abbreviated last name be switched to a full last name where first name like andrew. Note the following.

SQL command.

```
Declare
tempchar varchar2(25);
Begin
Select decode (lastname, 'IG', 'Igla')
into tempchar
from worker
where firstname like '%ndre%';
insert into temp (comments)
values            (tempchar);
exception
when NO_DATA_FOUND
insert into temp (comments)
values                   ('NO IG');
end;
```

Let us create an object worker_object. Note the following.

SQL command.

Create or replace type worker_object as object
              (ID number,
                firstname varchar2(25),
                lastname   varchar2(25));

Let us use object worker_object. Note the following.

SQL command.

```
Declare
p_worker_object    worker_object;
p_firstname        varchar2(25);
p_lastname         varchar2(25);
begin
p_firstname := 'andrew';
p_lastname := 'igla';
p_worker_object.lastname := p_lastname;
p-worker_object.firstname := p_firstname;
end;
```

An index is used in the following query teach%. An index would not be used if %teach were used in the following query. Note the following.

SQL command.

```
Declare
tempchar1  varchar2(25);
tempchar2  varchar2(25); Begin
Select decode (lastname, 'IG', 'Igla'), decode (firstname, 'andr',
'andrew')
into tempchar1, tempchar2
from worker
where worktype like 'maths teach%';
insert into temp  (comments1, comments2)
values            (tempchar1, tempchar2);
exception
when NO_DATA_FOUND
insert into temp (comments)
values                  ('NO Andrew igla maths teacher');
end;
```